Entc

f:

Author
Aaden M. Bruton-Smith

Ink to Legacy Publishing
Blythewood, SC

Ink to Legacy Publishing
PO Box 229
Blythewood, SC 29016

Cover Design by Tamell Green
Interior Design by Tamell Green
Edited by Jason Green

Special discounts are available on quantity purchases by corporations, associations, and others. For details, contact the author's manager at leslie@entourageyourself.com.

ENTOURAGE YOURSELF: KIDZ EDITION
Copyright © 2021 Aaden M. Bruton-Smith
Published by Ink to Legacy Publishing
Blythewood, South Carolina 29016

www.ink2legacy.com

ISBN 978-1-7363674-5-2 (pbk)

Library of Congress Control Number: 2021922476

Printed in the United States of America

Dedication

This book is dedicated to every boy or girl who has ever felt sad, alone, and overlooked. This book will help show you how strong you really are and how unique your purpose and life is. As you continue to love God and yourself, you will see just how special and important you and your purpose is in this world. This book is dedicated to young people like me, who are strong, powerful, and full of life and love.

We are the future
and
we make a difference
in the world!

Start Here

One of the most important voices that you will hear in life is the voice inside your head. Use Entourage Yourself books as a tool to help you magnify your inner voice and silence the outer voices around you. It is important that you know the power of your own thoughts and words. Also, it is important that you start as soon as possible in order to strengthen your spiritual muscles, so you will have the tools that you need to be victorious and channel your energy towards being the best version of yourself that you can be

I am so excited that you have chosen me to help encourage you along your journey! This book has daily readings that you can read for yourself or share with a friend. At the end of this book, you will find daily positive affirmations that I strongly suggest you speak and remember. Write these affirmations on a separate piece of paper and put them somewhere that you can see. Read them everyday.

Always remember you are loved you are important, and you matter!

Happy "You are a STAR" Sunday!

To be a star, you must shine brightly, follow your dreams, and never worry about how dark things around you may be. All you have to do is SHINE! Don't let darkness keep you from shining. Remember stars shine the brightest when they are in the dark. Be a guiding star to help others find their way. Be a shining star to light your own way. Keep shining; the world needs your light.

Never forget who you are, little star.

Spread the light! Live in light!
Speak in light! Be the light!

Write down ways that you can let your light shine.

Example: I can let my light shine by being kind to others.

1

2

3

4

5

6

7

8

9

10

5

Happy "Mistakes are a Part of Life" Monday!

No one is perfect. No one will ever be perfect. We all make mistakes at some point in life. It's a part of learning, growing, and discovering who you are as a person. Some mistakes will challenge you to change. Some mistakes will take longer to overcome. Some mistakes will show you what you are truly made of and how strong of a person you can be. Trust yourself and believe that the struggle that you may have faced today is developing the strength that you will need to face tomorrow. Don't be hard on yourself. Live. Love. Learn!

Making mistakes is part of life and a really big part of growing up, It's how you learn who you want to be.

Mistakes make your mind grow. Mistakes make your heart stronger. Mistakes make you wiser. Mistakes will be your best teacher, if you learn to apply the things you learned from the experience.

What is a mistake that you have made that has helped you grow as a person?

_____

_____

_____

_____

_____

_____

_____

_____

_____

Happy "Be Thoughtful" Tuesday!

Don't ever underestimate the power of a hug, smile, kind word, or listening ear. Stand up to a bully. Be a good friend. Take out the trash. Be kind to your siblings. Ask your mom or dad if they need help with anything around the house. Find a way to be helpful. Look for solutions instead of problems. Look for ways to use talents to help put a smile on someone else's face.

Never get tired of doing little things for others. Sometimes the little things matter the most.

Wherever there is a need, there is an opportunity for you to be the person to help.

What are some ways that you can be more thoughtful in your actions? What can you do more to help your family or friends?

_____

_____

_____

_____

_____

_____

_____

_____

_____

_____

Happy "What's Your Dream?" Wednesday!

No matter how big or small you think your dreams are, don't stop dreaming or thinking that you can achieve them. No matter what others think or say to you, don't stop trusting God for great things to happen to and for you! You are never too young to DREAM BIG! Dr. Martin Luther King had a dream that one day we would all be treated equally, fair, and right. He dreamed big no matter how bad the situation seemed to appear. If you can dream it, you can DO IT! Remember Philippians 4:13 declares, "I can do ALL things through Christ." DREAM BIG!

Every great dream begins with a dreamer.

You have to work hard. You have to fight. Always remain focused in order for your dreams to come true!

What do you desire to become? What are three dreams that you want to become your reality?

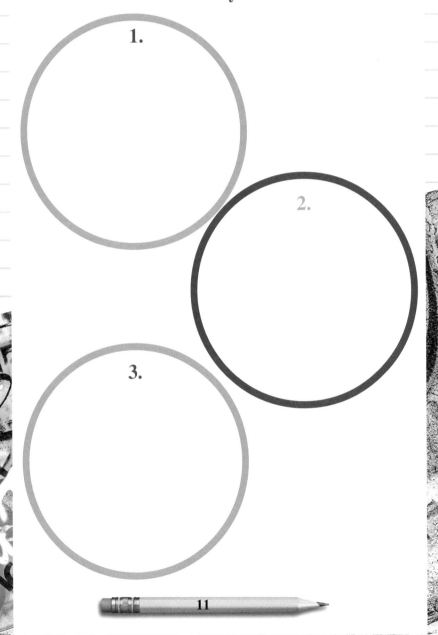

1.

2.

3.

Vision Board

On the next two pages create a vision board of the things you wrote down on page 11. You can cut out pictures in a magazine or download pictures from the internet then glue them here. Sometimes it helps to write things down and to see it everyday in order to reach your goals.

Vision Board

Happy "Think It Through" Thursday!

When you learn HOW to think and not WHAT to think, you will understand the power of your own thoughts. If you think too much, you may stress yourself out. If you think too little, you may miss the opportunity to be prepared. Overthinking can create anxiety and worry. Under-thinking can create unpreparedness. So, learn how to balance your thoughts so that you are not thinking too much or too little.

Think happy thoughts.

You have to think anyway, so think happy and creative thoughts. Meditate on thoughts that bring peace to your heart and mind.

What are you thinking right now? It does not have to make sense. It does not have to be positive or inspiring. Truthfully, write down your current thoughts, and then write something down that makes you feel happy when you think of it.

Happy "Forgiveness is Freedom" Friday!

We don't have control over how people treat us sometimes, but we do have control over how we respond to them all the time. People won't always be nice. They won't always have something kind to say. They won't always be friendly. There will be times when your feelings get hurt, and it won't always be intentional. Sometimes people will say things that make you sad; forgive them. People will do things to make you mad; forgive them. Forgiveness does not change the past, but it can always change the future.

Forgiveness is just another name for freedom.

Learn to forgive everyone for everything. Forgive them, even if they are not sorry. Holding on to anger only hurts you. It does not hurt them.

Has someone done something to you for which you have not offered your forgiveness? Why do you think it is important to forgive?

_____

_____

_____

_____

_____

_____

_____

_____

_____

_____

_____

Happy "Self-Love is the BEST Love" Saturday!

Love yourself right now just as you are. The only person that you need to ever compare yourself to is the person that you see when you look into the mirror. Be proud of who you are, and do not be ashamed of how other people view you. Don't ever doubt your worth. Don't ever question your abilities to do great and mighty things. A strong, positive self- image is a great start for achieving success in life.

Self-respect, self-worth, self-love, and self-confidence all begin with the word SELF. Don't look for any of those things outside of you.

You are good enough. You are smart. You are beautiful/handsome. You are strong. Believe it with all your heart, and don't let insecurities dictate your life.

Have you ever felt like you were not good enough? Did you ever feel not quite smart enough? Are there times when you do not feel strong enough? Do you still feel that way?

Write down three positive things about yourself and concentrate on those things.

Word Search

GOD   BOY   PRAY   AUTHENTIC

LIGHT   LOVE   GOALS   GIRL

FRIEND   FORGIVE   KIND   SHINING

LOOK UP, DOWN, & ACROSS FOR THESE WORDS

K	Z	G	C	U	G	B	G	O	D
I	K	O	J	S	I	P	K	C	F
N	T	A	D	F	R	I	E	N	D
D	M	L	E	O	L	N	C	J	B
E	C	S	V	R	B	H	H	P	M
T	H	D	O	G	E	K	D	R	I
Y	K	J	L	I	G	H	T	A	R
B	O	Y	U	V	C	F	Z	Y	R
A	U	T	H	E	N	T	I	C	O
S	H	I	N	I	N	G	O	X	R

Happy "Smile More" Sunday!

Surround yourself with people who make you smile more. Create moments and memories that make you laugh when you think back on them. Smile more than you cry. Give more than you take. Love more than you hate. You can bring positive energy into your daily life by smiling more and learning to find joy, even in the midst of sadness. Sometimes you may have to force yourself to smile, but in the end you make the world a better place when you can smile and be happy!

Nothing you wear is more important than your smile.

No matter how you are feeling, when you can smile and be happy, you open yourself up to healing!

21

Write down a time when you laughed so hard.

What makes you smile?

_____

_____

_____

_____

Happy "You MATTER" Monday!

Sometimes life has a way of making us feel unworthy or just not good enough. We compare our talents and abilities to those of other people, and we get down on ourselves when we feel like we are not like someone else. Well, guess what? You were not born to be like anyone else. You were born to do something in the world that only YOU can do. There is a purpose that only YOU can fulfill. No matter what you decide to do with your future, always remember that you are unique. You are special. You are worthy. You are loved.

There will always be someone who can't see your worth. Don't let that someone be YOU.

Sometimes in life you don't always feel important. On those days, remind yourself of how amazing you are! Sometimes the most important words that are spoken are the words that are spoken to yourself. YOU MATTER!

Have you ever felt unworthy or not important? Write about what happened. How can you look at things differently the next time you feel this way?

Have you ever felt unworthy or not important? Write about what happened. How can you look at things differently the next time you feel this way?

_____

_____

_____

_____

_____

_____

_____

_____

_____

_____

Happy "Be Thankful" Tuesday!

In all things, be thankful. In happy moments, be thankful. In difficult moments, be thankful. In quiet moments, be thankful. In painful moments, be thankful. When things are good, be thankful. When things are bad, be thankful. Be thankful for your family. Be thankful for your friends. Be thankful for your food. Be thankful for your home. Be thankful for your clothes. Be thankful for everything and everyone. There is someone in the world who wishes they had all the things that you have; so, be thankful.

There is always something for which to be thankful.

When you have a heart of thankfulness, God will give you more for which to be thankful.

Write down things and people for which you are thankful. Every day when you wake up, get up with a thankful heart and mind. Thank God for life every single day.

_____

_____

_____

_____

_____

_____

_____

_____

_____

_____

_____

Happy "Wisdom Will Guide You" Wednesday!

There will be so many times in your life that you will want to just speak whatever comes to your mind, but when you have the wisdom of God, He will give you the ability to know what to say and when to say it. Wisdom will help you make good decisions. Wisdom will keep you from getting yourself into trouble. Wisdom will teach you to choose to look at a situation from a different point of view. Wisdom is to your soul what health is to your body. Wisdom is to your mind what strength is to your muscles. Wisdom is to your heart what peace is to your being. Pray and ask God to not only let you be smart but to also be WISE!

Knowledge is knowing what
to say.
WISDOM
is knowing when to say it.

Pray this prayer:

God, give me a wise heart, mind, and spirit to be able to see what is good and what is evil. Give me the wisdom to know how to choose friends and how to choose which direction my life should take.

Amen.

Who is a wise person in your life from whom you can receive good advice? What has this person taught you that can help you be a good person in life?

_____

_____

_____

_____

_____

_____

_____

_____

_____

_____

Happy "Teachable Spirits are Growing Spirits" Thursday!

A teachable spirit is one that chooses to continue to learn, no matter their age or experience. There are so many valuable lessons that you will learn during your lifetime. You don't stop learning when you finish school. Life is like school, and experiences will often be your greatest teacher. Always seek knowledge and truth in order to grow in wisdom, humility, and excellence.

Be humble, teachable, and always keep learning.

You will never know it all. You will never have all the answers, but as long as you remain teachable, your spirit will continue to grow as you grow, too. Always strive for progress because you will never reach perfection.

Has there ever been a time where someone was trying to teach you something, and you didn't want to listen because you wanted to do it your way? What did you learn from that experience? If you've never experienced that, has there been a time where you were trying to teach someone something, but they didn't want to learn? Discuss that time.

_____

_____

_____

_____

_____

_____

_____

_____

_____

Happy "Have FUN" Friday!

It's very important to take life and your goals seriously, but it's just as important to be a KID and HAVE FUN! Life is too short to not have fun. Fun doesn't always have to be going to a park or going on a vacation. Create fun moments right where you are. There are times when you will lose sight of what's most important in life; life is better when you take the time to let loose and have fun.

Sometimes having FUN is all that you need.

Even though you're growing up, you should never stop doing things that bring you joy; never stop having FUN!

What do you like to do for fun? What is something that brings you joy?

Happy "Shine Brightly" Saturday!

Let your unique light shine. Let your weird light shine. Let your smart light shine. Let your leader light shine. Let your bright light shine. People will try to dim your light in several ways. They will tell you that your light is too bright. They will say that your light hurts their eyes. No matter what anyone says, God gave you the light that you have, so LET IT SHINE!

Let nothing dim the light that shines from within.

Let your light shine so brightly that others can see their way out of the dark by following the brightness of your light! Remember when you can't see your way, turn on your inner light!

Have you ever been really good at doing something, and you stop shining your light because of other people? What do you know now that you didn't know before that will help you keep shining your light, even if someone tries to dim it?

Word Search

JOY   FACE   HUMBLE   GRACE
CREATIVE   DANCE   FOREVER   MERCY
SUN   FUN   ADVICE   GIFT

LOOK UP, DOWN, & ACROSS FOR THESE WORDS

G	R	A	C	E	G	B	G	F	B
J	K	O	J	S	I	P	K	A	F
O	T	A	D	V	I	C	E	C	O
Y	M	E	R	C	Y	U	C	E	R
C	C	S	V	G	I	F	T	P	E
N	F	U	N	Y	E	K	D	R	V
A	K	C	R	E	A	T	I	V	E
D	A	N	C	E	C	F	Z	Y	R
M	S	U	N	E	T	Q	I	S	O
H	U	M	B	L	E	L	O	X	R

Happy" Self-Talk" Sunday!

It's not always what we say out loud that really determines our lives. It is the thing that we whisper to ourselves that has the most power. Positive self-talk is the key to being able to silence the voices of other people and magnify the voice of your heart. Self-talk is one of the most powerful forms of communication because it has the ability to defeat and discourage you or either encourage and empower you. Your mind will believe the things that you speak to it, so make sure you are speaking things that are lovely, true, noble, honest, positive, and good.

Self-talk is the most powerful form of communication because it either empowers you or it defeats you.

Be careful how you are talking to yourself, because you are listening."

–Lisa M. Hayes

Write down some positive things that you can say every day to yourself.

Happy "Manners Matter" Monday!

Saying "Please" and "Thank You" is more than having good manners. It shows how polite and kind you are at the core of your being. Good manners and a good attitude will open doors for you that you can't open on your own. If you are a pretty or handsome person with a bad attitude and bad manners, it makes your spirit ugly. You won't be as good looking as you can be. Having good manners sometimes is remaining kind and nice with people who don't always use their manners as well. Sometimes the prettiest thing a person can put on is a good smile and have good manners.

Your mood should not dictate your manners.

Thank you." "Please." "I'm sorry." "Excuse me." These are all good examples of using manners. Don't ever be rude to anyone, even when you are in a bad mood.

Has there ever been a time when someone was rude to you, and you still were nice anyway? What did you learn from that experience? How can you apply what you learned, if it ever happens again?

_____

_____

_____

_____

_____

_____

_____

_____

_____

_____

Happy "Trust Yourself" Tuesday!

Sometimes we can be our own biggest cheerleader and our own worst enemy. Your heart will guide you. Your mind will lead you. Your spirit will steer you in the right direction. Trust the voice in your mind and heart to lead you on the path that you must take. If you have a bad feeling about a friend and you feel like you should distance yourself, trust yourself. If you desire to become the next NBA player, trust yourself. If you want to become the next president, trust yourself. Trust yourself enough to know that you know enough to make a good decision for your future.

Trust yourself. You know more than you think you do.

Just trust your own voice. And keep exploring the things that are interesting to you.
-Nikki Giovanni

Do you ever doubt yourself to make a good decision? Why don't you trust yourself? What can you do to start trusting your voice more than the voice of other people?

_____

_____

_____

_____

_____

_____

_____

_____

_____

_____

Happy "Work Hard" Wednesday!

A dream doesn't become reality on its own; it takes determination and hard work to make your dreams come true. Things won't happen overnight, but you must be dedicated and committed to reach your goals in life. It won't always be an easy journey, but God will give you the strength that you need to make it when times get hard. In the moments when it does get hard, it doesn't mean that you quit or slow down. It means that you must stay even more focused on your goals and not be distracted, no matter what. It will not be easy, but it will be worth it in the end!

You get what you work for, not for what you wish.

Work hard in silence, and let your success make the noise.

Has there ever been a time where you wanted to achieve something, and it became hard and you wanted to quit trying? What did you learn from that experience?

_____

_____

_____

_____

_____

_____

_____

_____

_____

_____

_____

Happy "Try Again" Thursday!

Don't be scared of failure. Learn from it and continue trying. Don't be discouraged by not being successful the first time that you try something. You may not always get it right the first time around. Failing is not an option, but LEARNING always is. So, take a deep breath. Hold your head up. TRY AGAIN!

If at first you don't succeed, try, try again!

You only fail when you stop trying. So, don't ever stop trying to find a way to be successful at what you are attempting. Even if you have to try over and over, do it! Just keep going!

Have you ever been so frustrated with doing something new that you gave up on trying? Did you try again? If so, did you succeed eventually? If not, go ahead and give it another try. No matter what, don't give up!

_____

_____

_____

_____

_____

_____

_____

_____

_____

_____

Happy "Focus on the Good" Friday!

Stay focused on your dreams and goals by ignoring distractions that will try to hinder you from being the best version of yourself. Your life will move in the direction of your focus, so if you focus on negative things you will have a negative life. If you focus on positivity, then positivity will follow you in all areas of your life. The key to being a positive person is focusing on your goals and not your obstacles. If you ever have a day when you are not focused, don't worry. Get back on track by changing the channel in your mind.

Focus on your goals, not your fears."

Don't be hard on yourself for not being a perfect person. You will lose focus from time to time, but you simply need a positive thought to get back on track.

In the moments when you lose focus, what can you do to get back on track?

Happy "Share Your Story" Saturday!

Don't hold back from sharing your story with someone. You never know how you can inspire or help someone to start to write or rewrite a part of their story by listening to your story. One of the most powerful parts of your body is your mind. Your mind holds stories of the past and possibilities of the future. Don't hold back on how you feel and what you have been through because you can possibly help someone overcome an obstacle or challenge. Live in your truth and express your thoughts. Don't be ashamed to share your truth.

Never be afraid to share your story

Every life has a purpose. Share your story, and you may help someone find their voice to share his or her story, too.

Has a friend ever told you something about what they have been through, and you were able to relate to what they shared? How can you help a friend who has been through a situation that you have experienced?

Word Search

MOVE   SUPER   FAMILY   STRONG
FINISH   HAPPY   EPIC   START
FEAR   TRUTH   HEART   JESUS

LOOK UP, DOWN, & ACROSS FOR THESE WORDS

S	U	R	E	L	O	W	G	H	J
U	S	A	P	M	T	N	A	S	E
P	T	O	I	Y	D	P	Q	T	S
E	A	Y	C	U	P	X	C	R	U
R	R	V	V	Y	B	M	Y	O	S
H	T	R	U	T	H	B	U	N	D
F	E	A	R	J	R	O	M	G	E
H	E	A	R	T	T	L	D	A	V
F	A	M	I	L	Y	D	H	Y	O
F	B	F	I	N	I	S	H	J	M

Happy "Start Strong, Finish Stronger" Sunday!

If you're brave enough to start, you're strong enough to finish it all the way to the end. Remember, you have more potential than you believe that you do. Don't start something and then get stuck in the middle because things may become difficult in the process. You may have started out strong and lost your motivation. In those moments, you feel like you are going to quit. Keep this in mind: fight the fight. Finish the race. Keep the faith. Keep going. You don't have to be the person to always finish first, but you do have to be the person to at least FINISH!

Starting strong is good. Finishing strong is epic.

Be the type of person that finishes what he or she starts. Don't get weary or discouraged when things get hard. Use those moments as reminders to channel all your energy to finishing stronger than you started. Remember, you can do ALL things through Christ who gives you strength.

Is there something (hobby, sports, school work, chores, etc.) that you have started, and because you became overwhelmed, you quit? What will you do the next time you are in this type of situation?

Happy "Move Forward" Monday!

Life is about learning, loving, and staying in a place of always moving forward. Sometimes when we make mistakes, or when we are upset about something, it's hard to move ahead in our minds. One thing you have to always remember is that every day we get a new day. Each new day comes with an opportunity to move beyond any feelings of anger, disappointment, and sadness.

Keep moving forward.

Don't let anything stop you from moving ahead. Don't let the disappointment of yesterday keep you from enjoying the joy, happiness, and peace of today!

Write down a quote that can help you move forward in moments when you want to give up.

Happy "There are NO Limits" Tuesday!

God has blessed us with the ability to dream. He has given us the amazing capability to believe in the power of our own dreams. The only real limitation on your abilities is the level of your desire to achieve your goals. If you want it badly enough, there is nothing or no one that can stop you from reaching what you want to achieve. If you can get your mind to line up with your heart to believe God for the impossible, He will give you the strength to achieve ANYTHING that you want to do.

The only limits in life are the ones that YOU make.

The only limit you will ever have is the one that you have created in your mind. Train your brain to trust God for the impossible!

Write down three life goals that you want to accomplish. Don't limit yourself.
DREAM BIG!

57

Happy "Winners Don't Quit" Wednesday!

You have to fight through some hard and tough days in order to appreciate the value of the good days. Success in life comes when you refuse to give up, no matter what obstacles come your way. Stay strong and always remain positive. You will struggle at some point in your life, but know that struggles only come to make you stronger. Believe in yourself. Believe in your dreams. Believe in the power of God, and know that you will reap a reward if you never give up.

If you get tired, learn to rest but don't quit.

The difference in winning and losing is most often not quitting.

-Walt Disney

Have you ever quit doing something that you really wanted to do, but you were frustrated with the process? What can you do the next time you feel like quitting in order to help keep you motivated on reaching your goals?

_____

_____

_____

_____

_____

_____

_____

_____

_____

_____

_____

Happy "Think Before You Speak" Thursday!

Words are powerful. They can create joy, or they can destroy joy. Choose what you say before you say it. Your tongue is a powerful tool, and the words we say may be forgiven, but they are never forgotten. So, be mindful of what you allow to come out of your mouth before you say it. Sometimes you speak from a place of frustration, but learn how to control your tongue. Sometimes you speak from a place of anger, but learn how to manage your emotions. Sometimes you speak from a place of sadness, but learn to speak your truth without holding back how you really feel. Words are free, but it's how you use them that may cost you.

Think before you speak. Words can hurt.

Words are powerful weapons. We should think of the consequences before we aim them at other people.
-Susan Gale

Have you ever said something to someone, and after you said it, you wished you could have taken it back? What did you learn from that experience? Has someone ever said something to you that you wish they didn't say? How did that help you learn to be mindful of your words?

Happy "Friends are Important" Friday!

F. R. I. E. N. D. S

Forgive you when you make a mistake

Respect you

Include you

Encourage you

Need you like you need them

Don't hurt you on purpose

Stand by your side

Good friends are like stars. You can't always see them, but you know that they are always there.

Friendship is like a beautiful garden. The more you water and take care of your friends, the more the friendship will grow. Friendship is a joint effort. You should get out what you put into it. Be a good friend and make sure your friends are being a good friend to you!

Do you have best friends? What are their names? What are your favorite things to do with your friends?

_____

_____

_____

_____

_____

_____

_____

_____

_____

_____

_____

Happy "Success Starts with YOU" Saturday!

Your happiness and success in life all lies and begins with you. If you tell yourself that you can't do it, then you won't do it. When you think about quitting something that you started, always remember the reason why you started so that it can motivate you to keep at it. Winston Churchill once said, "Success is not final. Failure is not fatal; it is the courage to continue that counts." Success won't come to you. You must go to it!

All success begins with self-discipline. It starts with you.

Don't let what you can't do stop you from doing the things that you are capable of doing.

Write down three of your successes? Think about how they made you feel.

Happy "Self-Respect" Sunday!

What does it mean to have self-respect? It can be defined as knowing when you are good and worthy of being treated well, kindly, and with love. It's when you have confidence in yourself. When you respect yourself, you are giving a demand for others to treat you with respect as well. It is never too early to learn the value and importance of self-respect. Having self-respect is also having respect for others, no matter how disrespectful that person may be. Whatever you believe about yourself on the inside will be manifested to you on the outside.

The way you treat yourself sets the standard for how others will treat you, too.

If you don't see your worth and value, you will choose people who won't always see your worth and value either.

In your own words, what do you think it means to have self-respect?

_____

_____

_____

_____

_____

_____

_____

_____

_____

_____

_____

_____

Happy "Mindset Check" Monday!

You have the ability to make a bad situation good and the ability to make a good situation bad by the thoughts that go through your mind. Your mindset is what you have chosen to believe about something. You can see the good, or you can see the bad. You can look at the glass as being half empty, or you can look at the glass being half full. You change your mindset by changing the language that you speak to yourself about yourself. You change your mindset by learning from mistakes and applying the lessons that you have learned. You change your mindset by creating new habits that support the change you desire to have and surrounding yourself around friends that match the mindset you desire to have. You can have a fixed mindset, which means you don't want to change because you are okay with how things are, or you can choose to have a growth mindset. A growth mindset means you desire to work to always grow and become better. The choice is up to you.

Your life is as good as your mindset

Write five pieces of advice that have been given to you to help grow your mindset.

Happy "Talk to God Every Day" Tuesday!

Before you sleep, PRAY! When you wake up, PRAY! When life gets hard, PRAY! When you're happy, PRAY! If you're happy, PRAY! If you're unsure, PRAY! God is always with us. He always hears us. Don't wait until you are in trouble to pray. Prayer is simply a conversation with God. God loves for you to talk to Him. The most important conversation that you will have every day is the conversation that you have with God.

With or without problems, learn to always talk to God.
-Ravinder Malik

God has no phone, but you still can call Him. He doesn't have Facebook, but He still is your friend. He doesn't have Snapchat or TikTok, but you can still follow Him.

Do you find it difficult to pray? If so, why?
What are three main things that you want God
to know about? Write them down.

_____

_____

_____

_____

_____

_____

_____

_____

_____

_____

_____

_____

Happy "Wealth Isn't Always Money" Wednesday!

Wealth is not how much money that you have. Wealth is being healthy. Wealth is having knowledge. Wealth is having peace. Wealth is having food and shelter. Wealth is having love. There are so many ways to be wealthy without having a lot of money. The real measure of your wealth is how much you will be worth if you had no money. The real measure of your wealth is knowing who you are without having to prove your value in material possessions.

You are too brilliant to be broke.
–Daphne D. Williams

You aren't wealthy until you have something that money can't buy.

Do you know a wealthy person (not in money but in knowledge, information, love, things that you can't physically touch)? Who is this person, and what have they taught you that you can apply to your daily life?

_____

_____

_____

_____

_____

_____

_____

_____

_____

_____

Happy "Turn Away from Toxic People" Thursday!

Don't ever apologize for standing up for yourself and pulling away from people who are toxic to your growth and development. Here's a short list of traits of a toxic person:

- Those who bully you or others
- Those who are always negative
- Those who are jealous of you
- Those who are self-centered
- Those who disappoint you
- Those who criticize you and never have positive things to say to you

Friends are supposed to lift you up. They are supposed to encourage you. Friends are supposed to pray for you and wish you well in life. If you have a friend who is not helping you to become a better person, then you need to find a new friend.

Removing toxic people from your life isn't selfish, its survival.

Don't ever think it is okay for a person to be mean to you. Stand up for yourself, even if standing up means you walk away from being that person's friend.

Have you ever experienced being friends with someone who hasn't always been nice to you? Are you still friends with that person? Are they a better friend now?

_____

_____

_____

_____

_____

_____

_____

_____

_____

_____

_____

Happy "No Fear" Friday!

Remember God has not given us the spirit of fear (Read 2 Timothy 1:7). No matter what, do not let the fear of what could go wrong keep you from trying to do something you are afraid to do. Being brave isn't always not feeling fear; being brave is having the feeling and finding a way to get through it. Sometimes the things we don't understand cause us to be fearful. Wake up everyday stronger than yesterday. Face your fears and wipe your tears.

Fear kills more dreams than failure ever will.

Don't let fear keep you from making decisions.

What are you afraid of? Have you spoken to your parents about those things that make you fearful?

_____

_____

_____

_____

_____

_____

_____

_____

_____

_____

_____

Happy "Self-Esteem is Super Important" Saturday!

- Don't compare yourself to others.
- Don't be afraid to be yourself.
- Don't think you have to do what everyone else is doing.
- Identify your needs, hopes, and wants and make good choices towards those things.
- Talk to yourself like you would talk to your best friend; say good things to yourself.
- Connect with others who treat you the way you deserve to be treated.
- Create boundaries.
- Laugh.
- Play.
- Have FUN!
- Focus on your efforts and learn from mistakes.
- Don't worry about things you can't control.

Repeat this three times:
I am fearless.
I am strong.
I can do anything.

(Build your self-esteem.)

How do you view yourself? Do you think you are a good person? When you make a mistake, are you hard on yourself, or do you give yourself a chance to learn and grow?

_____

_____

_____

_____

_____

_____

_____

_____

_____

_____

_____

Word Search

SMART   DECISIONS   CAN   HARD
GROW   LEARN   SELF   FOCUS
BORN   LEADER   DO   LAUGH

LOOK UP, DOWN, & ACROSS FOR THESE WORDS

S	M	A	R	T	O	W	G	H	D
R	S	A	P	F	O	C	U	S	O
S	T	O	I	Y	D	P	Q	T	L
E	A	Y	C	U	H	A	R	D	E
L	R	V	L	A	U	G	H	O	A
F	C	A	N	T	H	B	U	N	D
F	B	O	R	N	R	O	M	G	E
H	S	D	L	E	A	R	N	A	R
F	A	G	R	O	W	D	H	Y	O
D	E	C	I	S	I	O	N	S	M

Daily Affirmations

I am Smart.
I am Mighty.
I am Strong.
I make good decisions with friends.
I am a leader.
I am above.
I can do all things through Christ.
I am creative.
I am who God says that I am.
I will make a difference in the world.
I am grateful.
I control my own happiness.
I was born to be different.

About the Author

Hi! I'm Aaden Mekhi Bruton-Smith, native of Greenville, South Carolina. I am 12 years old, and I love to help people, I love to play basketball and I love my family and friends. I am very passionate about self-love and self-worth because I have experienced bullying from an adult as well as my peers. Through that experience and with the love and support of my family and true friends, I overcame those moments and became a stronger and better person. My favorite bible verse is, "I can do all things through Christ that strengthens me…Philippians 4:13" I believe that with God, all things are possible. I hope you enjoy reading my book and I pray that you find encouragement and hope every day.

Thank You to my amazing parents, Leslie K. Bruton and Michael T. Smith for always showing me the right way, loving and guiding me and introducing me to God and the importance of prayer.

Thank you to my Godmother, Tiffany T. Jones, for always believing in me and being there when I need it the most.

Thank you to every person who has helped me find my worth and value in this world. I appreciate you.

Stay in connection with me by following me on IG @aadenbrutonsmith2k27_.